Back Country Treks on Grapevine Mesa

Mary McBee

Friends of Arizona Joshua Tree Forest

Meadview, Arizona

Back Country Treks on Grapevine Mesa

© Copyright 2019 Mary McBee

Updated April 2019

Cover photo: Storm at sunset as viewed through the Elephant Arch, with Gregg Basin on Lake Mead in background, 1986, by Mary McBee

All photos in this work by author unless otherwise credited. Specific hike sketches by author.

Library of Congress Cataloging-in-publication data:

McBee, Mary Richardson

Back Country Treks on Grapevine Mesa

Includes maps, sketches, and photos.

ISBN-13: 978-0-578-44168-9

1. McBee, Mary 2. Lake Mead 3. Grapevine Mesa 4. Meadview, AZ.
5. Lake Mead National Recreation Area 6. Hiking at Lake Mead

Friends of Arizona Joshua Tree Forest

Meadview, Arizona

arizonajoshuatreeforest.org

arizonajoshuatreeforest@gmail.com

While every effort has been made to assure the accuracy of the information in this book, by using this book you take full responsibility for your own safety and recognize that outdoor activities may be hazardous.

Acknowledgments

Larry Townsend provided excellent assistance with the main area map design and computer workings and Vern Farris assisted with information and proofing. My daughter, Suzanne Wanatee Buffalo, helped with proofing and put the final draft into presentable computerized form. All photos were from my own collection unless credited otherwise. I take sole responsibility for the hand-drawn sketches of each hike. Mary McBee, February 2014

Update: Spring, 2018. As I did not finish publishing this booklet, the Friends of Arizona Joshua Forest on Grapevine Mesa has taken on the task and with the help of Bruce Grubbs in Flagstaff, is completing publication of this work. All proceeds of sales will therefore go to the benefit of this group and the fine work they are doing to help preserve the magnificent Joshua Forest on the mesa.

Contents

Section One: Grapevine Mesa West

Section Two: Grapevine Mesa East

Area Map and Legend

1 - Boundary, Lake Mead Nat'l Recreation Area

2 - Town of Meadview

3 - Scenic Overlook

4 - Ranger Station

5 - Pearce Ferry Road

6 - South Cove Road

7 - South Cove

8 - Sandy Point

9 - Wheeler Ridge

10 - Pearce Ferry Landing

11 - Western Entrance to Grand Canyon

12 - Grapevine Wash

13 - Hualapai Wash

14 - Hualapai Bay

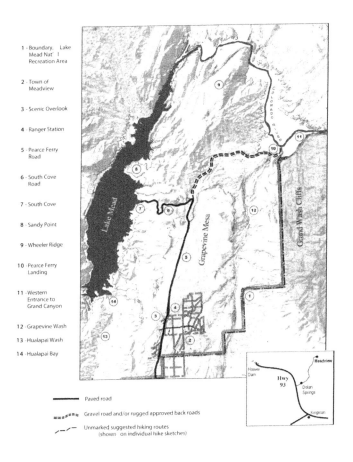

—————— Paved road

═ ═ ═ ═ Gravel road and/or rugged approved back roads

– – – Unmarked suggested hiking routes
(shown on individual hike sketches)

Introduction

The information given in this booklet has purposely been left somewhat vague, this to encourage the joy of exploration, the delight of making one's own discoveries. Other than providing an initial area map, additional resources such as topographical maps, gps locations, or satellite views are NOT referenced. All distances given are just best guesses. Simple sketch maps accompany each hike, however, these sketches do not provide accurate distances or accurate detail regarding terrain. They only point you in the direction of interesting places. When giving directions, I occasionally referred to the National Park Service's 'Approved Backroads Map' regarding rugged 4 wheel-drive back roads. If you are not familiar with these, go to the Lake Mead National Recreation Area site and pull up the Temple Bar Area Approved Backroads Map. There you'll see that the right half of the Temple Bar Area section shows the Meadview/Grapevine Mesa area.

www.nps.gov/lake/planyourvisit/upload/Approved-Backcountry-Road-Map-Temple-Bar-2016.pdf.

Nearly all these wonderful remote places are ones I discovered when living in this area decades ago, partially during the early 1970's, but mainly while exploring every nook and cranny I could find during the 1980's. Over the years and decades since, I've shared these discoveries with many friends. You'll notice most of these explorations involve walking 'down' since a lifetime of arthritis determined this my best means of travel. If you'd rather go 'up,' then start at the opposite end, or, if a hardy hiker, go both ways, or find a more circuitous route of your own and discover new ways.

Several places referenced herein were already known by a few old-timers when I arrived on the mesa in the early 70's; the petroglyphs along the Old Wagon Road, the two oft-visited ancient roasting pits near Lucky Seven Corral, and of course, beautiful Grapevine Springs. Few, however, knew anything of the other unique gems described. Abundant sign is evident that Native Americans had already been pretty much everywhere.

One issue for hikers might be finding an NPS acceptable space to park a vehicle while hiking in the back country here without offending rangers or local deputies. For day hikes, usually a note on your windshield quells concerns if you're parked sufficiently off the main route of travel and yet not destroying any vegetation (quote: LMNRA Supt Dickinson, 3/28/12). To leave a vehicle parked overnight, however, try to find an area ranger (or some way to contact one) in order to learn current preferences as these change with ever-changing personnel. No vehicular travel off the Approved Backroads are allowed within LMNRA boundaries. Respect these rules. They are for good reason.

Most of the explorations described involve walking to places that neither vehicles nor ATV's can access. However, there are a number of interesting approved back roads accessible and enjoyed by 4 x 4's and ATV's, and I often had the good fortune to have friends and family who would meet me with their boat at the end of jaunts down to the lake or river, or with their 4 x 4 on land. Most of the information in this booklet, however, is for those who want to walk where vehicles simply cannot go. Remote is the word. Yet one would have to make great effort to get lost in this mesa country. There are landmarks visible from everywhere, with the majestic Grand Wash Cliffs to the east and sprawling Lake Mead to the west, these allowing one to easily retain bearings.

Intriguing history exists about this unique and little-known area, one that for centuries served as the major western trade route around the Grand Canyon for prehistoric people, then later, for historic peoples. Extensive and in-depth historical information on this is covered on this entire area and I highly recommend digging into the research work done in this regard, *A Deep Map of Western Grand Canyon and Upper Lake Mead Area*, by myself, under the author name of Mary Richardson McBee. The book is available for sale through both the Meadview Chamber of Commerce and Amazon and is in various libraries.

Only a few great hikes will be introduced here. There are many other places to explore. One can park up at the old airstrip on the north end of Grapevine Mesa (visible from

Meadview), have a picnic at the Pearce Ferry overlook and simply stroll along that rim. Or, explore onto one of the twin buttes on each side of the upper part of South Cove Road, these the locals call the North and South Monolith. One can park down at Pearce Ferry landing and walk in many directions, along the river/lake, or park along Pearce Ferry gravel road and hike into the more remote Wheeler Ridge area to the north. There are additional side canyons in Grapevine Wash wonderful to explore. There are more routes from the western rim of Grapevine Mesa and down to the lake not identified here. I found three ways down off the rim from on top of Grand Wash Cliffs. Or you can simply wander along some back roads, for example, walk down the Golden Gate Mine road (Rd. # 142).

It is very important to note that this guide does not encompass the wonderfully unique Joshua Forest Reserve and related trails on the higher and more southern end of Grapevine Mesa. A separate brochure and information is in the works by others to provide more specific information on this superb Joshua Forest area.

All the risks of hiking in this back country are your own.... yet, the surprises and delights are manifold. These rarely visited backcountry lands are all managed by the National Park Service yet mandated with more multiple-use than those within National Parks. This means on this recreation land you can walk wherever you want, whenever you want. No permits are required, no fee's levied. There are few if any trails, try your best not to leave any, nor any markings. Hike alone if you desire (by far the most rewarding for me in spite of numerous warnings). Go with friends if you desire.

The singular beauty and unique isolation in remote areas of this mesa are precious, the landscapes exquisite. Come to know this land. Come to respect and love this land.

Mary McBee 2012, 2018

Sharon by a large Joshua Tree in the Joshua Forest on Grapevine Mesa

4

Section One: Grapevine Mesa West

From the lengthy west rim of Grapevine Mesa overlooking Lake Mead, there are a labyrinth of great canyons to hike. Most of them can be explored without ropes or rock climbing expertise, but not all. If you find yourself in a place where you don't feel safe, turn around and walk back out. Many of these hikes are most fun to explore if you have a ride waiting at the bottom, either a boat or 4 x 4 vehicle. For hardier hikers, make the round trip. I'll also mention a few interesting shorter walks that lay just off the paved and gravel sections of Pearce Ferry Road; specifically, the Tinaja, Turtle Rock Sink, and Elephant Arch.

The Tinaja and Mesa Rim

This is the easiest hike in this little guide, and indeed, simply parking any place along Pearce Ferry Road between the Ranger Station at Meadview (milepost 39) and the Airstrip Road entrance four miles farther north and then hiking from Pearce Ferry Road over to the Grapevine Mesa Rim is delightful and most relaxing, with a view from the rim that is gorgeous. This area is quite level and not more than about 1/4-1/2 mile in distance to the rim, depending where you hike.

Tinaja is a Spanish term often used to describe natural water cachements in rocks that occur in desert terrains. The Tinaja I found on our mesa is a large boulder with a shallow cachement, one usually only containing water during the winter months or immediately after rain. Needless to say, when it does contain water, many animal signs are present around the rock.

Directions

On Pearce Ferry Road, go north 1.7 miles beyond the Scenic Overlook and Ranger Station. Just BEFORE you get to milepost 42 (yet when 42 post is visible), there's a large boulder on the left side of the road and a pull-out on the right where you can park. Look west (left) toward the mesa rim. You'll see a rise on the rim that's somewhat 'behind' the others and looks more barren. I call this 'bald knob' and often found bighorn at that great look-out, but rarely since 2000. Walk directly toward the bald knob and just a tad to the left. When you get about 1/3 way to the rim (440 paces, to be more exact), keep your eyes open for a large flat rock situated on a low rise.

After you find the Tinaja (or don't), walk on over to the rim. It's a most inspiring view.

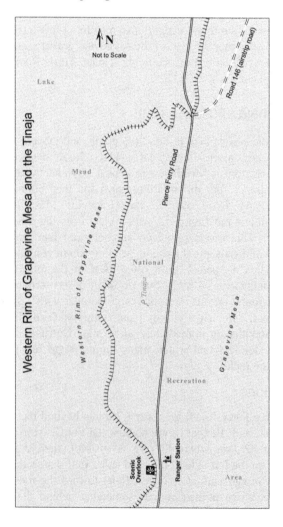

View from Bald Knob on the Mesa Rim, 2010

The Tinaja, 2010

Locals at Natural Tinaja on mesa

George at the Tinaja

Wonder Canyon

Wonder and Tortoise Canyons are beautiful "twin canyons" paralleling each other just north of the South Cove Road. They are magnificent finds and have long been two of my favorite mesa hikes since stumbling upon them in the 1980's.

Most hikers prefer to leave a car down at the South Cove parking area, then park another up at the pull-out at the intersection of Pearce Ferry Road and South Cove in order to only hike this one way. Wonder is approximately 5-6 miles in distance, depending how one exits at the lower end. This can be considered a moderate to difficult hike, depending on a hikers abilities as both these canyons require some degree of rock scrambling around some steep dryfalls, but none that require ropes. I named this first one "Wonder" because it continued to present unique surprises and beauty at nearly every turn, not to mention, I was surprised to simply be able to get on through and exit the lower end.

Directions

After parking at the intersection of Pearce Ferry Road and South Cove Road, hike up the bluff on the west side of the parking area toward the "twin buttes" (some call monoliths), then follow that ridge northwesterly and as it curves some to the right. You'll soon see three ridges descending from that ridge to the west (left). Continue on until you reach the last descending ridge that has a large "split rock" boulder toward the lower end and follow that ridge down toward the lake. After passing the split rock and reaching the wash at the bottom, continue straight west and this will lead you down into the entrance of Wonder Canyon.

As you enter the canyon, there will be a few small dryfalls to negotiate but none difficult. About half-way through the canyon, however, you'll come to a narrows and then a sheer dryfall. Back up a bit and go up around on the reddish bench on the right. Stay up on the bench for a time as there's another large dryfall in the wash just below the first one, then work back down into the wash which soon broadens out. From there on, follow the large wash down to the lake.

If your car is parked at South Cove, you can get there two ways: by hiking across ridges and washes in the direction of South Cove Rpad just after returning into the large wash bed, or, upon reaching the lake, hike back across ridges and washes from there over to South Cove. Better yet, have a friend meet you with a boat in South Bay. South Bay is on the south side of Sandy Point, the large sandy peninsula that juts out into the lake just north of South Cove ramp.

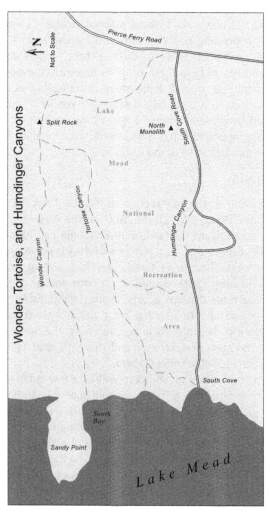

George in Wonder Canyon, 2012

Tom Christoffer above large dry fall area in Wonder, 2009

Locals coming through Wonder Canyon

Tortoise Canyon

Follow the same general direction for parking and entering as for Wonder Canyon given just previous. I named this one Tortoise as upon descending into this beautiful canyon the first time, I found a huge desert tortoise shell in the wash bed near the entrance. After taking a group of locals through here in 2011, they began calling it Seven Falls Canyon.

Tortoise is a bit shorter than Wonder, about four miles, depending where one exits at the lower end. This could also be considered moderate to somewhat difficult as one dryfall does require some rock scrambling to bypass.

Directions

Leave your pick-up vehicle either down at the South Cove parking lot or at one of the pull-outs just below milepost three on South Cove Road. Then start at the intersection of Pearce Ferry Road and South Cove Road, following the same walking directions as for Wonder Canyon.

After following the same ridge approach as to Wonder Canyon, and after you pass the split-rock boulder at the lower end of the third ridge going down (west) into the wash bed, rather than continue straight on into Wonder, veer south (left) and follow that wash until it curves back west (right) and that takes you down into Tortoise Canyon. You'll clamber over a few short dryfalls, then in the upper part of that canyon, you'll find a narrows and a sheer dryfall. You can scramble up a fairly steep short scree slope to the right and then down over some large boulders to return into the wash bed. From there on, you'll continue down and only encounter dryfalls that are relatively easy to work around.

Upon exiting the main part of the canyon, one can work to the left (south) and go over to the South Cove Road if you have a car parked there. Otherwise, follow the wash on down toward the lake and work back over several ridges to return to the South Cove parking lot.

Entering Tortoise Canyon, 2010

By-passing early dry fall in canyon, 2010

Humdinger Canyon

This short little canyon was a startling surprise and not meant for the faint-hearted. I named this one Humdinger.

Interesting story follows. When my husband and I were stationed here during the early 1970's, our son and daughter, Dave and Suzanne, were in elementary school and rode the school bus 40 miles to Dolan Springs daily. In Meadview, they were great friends with the Huffer boys, Craig and Todd, of similar ages, and all four were full of adventure and exploration. When they would come dragging back home on various days, mentioning how they had walked down to Grapevine Springs and back (I didn't realize then that it was a good 12 miles in sand, during summer), or that they had found some cool dryfalls just off South Cove Road and had left a rope hanging over one of the falls that they couldn't retrieve; all that was before I had been doing much exploration myself and really had no understanding of how adventurous they actually had been.

In the early 1980's, when my own explorations began, one day I decided to explore an interesting-looking little short canyon just off South Cove Road. After scrambling around some boulders, I came to a deep dryfall, and there, still hanging ten years later, was the rope our young children had left behind. I was incredulous, stared at the falls, and then began wondering what kind of parent I had been.

This canyon is only about a quarter-mile long and turns out this barrier was the reason for the 's' curve halfway down South Cove Road. It has two major dryfalls, the first a beautiful convoluted slickrock fall, the second more of a sheer drop. Excellent climbers could get around them but most folks wouldn't want to try. With Humdinger being so accessible to South Cove Road, when I mentioned this little canyon to Don and Rick (our two resident Rangers), they and some of we volunteers soon began using these falls to practice rappelling.

Directions

Go about halfway down South Cove Road and just before proceeding through a big cut (after this is the 's curve'), park along right side of road and look down into the wash to the right. Work down through there into Humdinger. After exiting both dry falls, you will come back out on the lower part of South Cove Road.

Rangers Rick and Don, along with locals Ben, Dave, and Sharon, preparing to rappel down first dry fall in Humdinger Canyon

Don McBee rappelling in Humdinger Canyon

Ben rappelling in Humdinger Canyon

Old Wagon Road and Historic Wall

This is a moderate hike, qualifying as such only due to its length but with no rock scrambling or climbing around dryfalls. This is perhaps six miles one-way. It's nice to have someone with a boat meet you at the lake at the end of this hike.

There is much history behind this road and valley. The road was cut by William Gregg who was the first pioneer to homestead a ranch at a spring in the valley below in 1880, just south of South Cove. It was first called the Greggs Ranch (also Griggs), and then became known as the Smith Ranch when Williams two stepsons, Tom and Bill Smith, eventually took over the ranch. This ranch and spring were submerged under water when Lake Mead was formed in the early 1930's. (For more information on this river crossing, ranch, and family, see book mentioned in Introduction.)

Directions

Park at the scenic overlook on Grapevine Mesa/Meadview, across from the Ranger Station (just north of milepost 39 on Pearce Ferry Road). Walk to the left and follow the old Wagon Road down into the valley below. In the valley the road disappears, but keep heading northward in this wide valley -- don't turn left and follow a wash that leads you, instead, out into Smith Bay. Slowly the valley will close-in until you're walking in a rocky wash. As the wash closes in more (still heading north), keep your eye on the light-colored wall that begins to appear along the right side. All along this wall there are very old faded petroglyphs, also layered with drawings by miners and the historic 'Tom and Fay' signature (Tom Smith and his wife, Fay). After that wall, the wash turns left and goes on down to the lake, coming out into Wagon Trail Bay. Along the hill on the southern side of the bay, you can still distinctly see part of the old road.

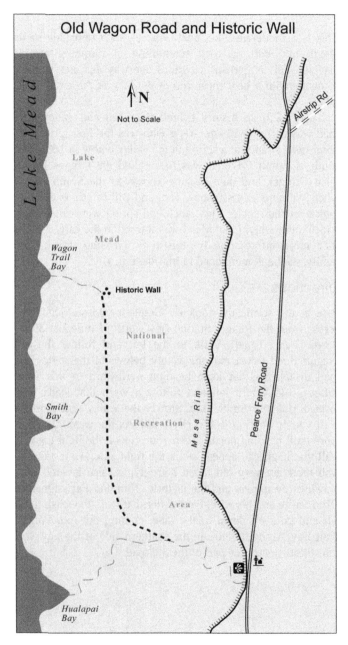

Group viewing petroglyphs area, 2011. Photo by Sharon Baur

Fay and Tom (Smith) old signature and petroglyphs along Old Wagon Trail Road

Elephant Arch

This is an easy to moderate interesting short hike just off Grapevine Mesa rim toward the lake, one a person can do in an hour or less. I discovered this unique arch in the mid-1980's. After taking friends, Ron and Sharon, down to see it a few months later and as we approached during the early morning hours, sunlight from the east shown down on the arch, beautifully defining the outline. Ron exclaimed.... 'It looks like an elephant!' And it is so-named.

Directions

On Pearce Ferry Road in Meadview, about half-way between the street corners of Meadview Blvd and Hualapai Creek Drive (just south of the Scenic Overlook), note of a short little gravel road that goes off to the rim. Drive out there and park. Walk just a bit to the north (right) and you'll top out on three ridges that go down toward a lengthy rock outcropping or ledge below. Take the most southerly (left) ridge down and as you approach the ledge below, look to your right and you'll see the Elephant Arch. Take time to explore this unique formation.

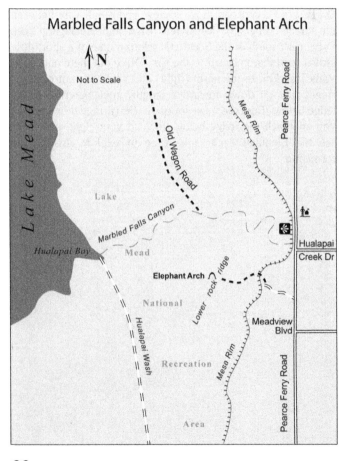

Marbled Falls Canyon and Elephant Arch

Distant view of Elephant Arch

27

Elephant Arch viewed from above

Marbled Falls Canyon

This delightful little trek leads one to the eloquent silver-blue Marbled Falls not seen by many who even reside on Grapevine Mesa. Most of this hike would be considered moderate except for the effort required going around its namesake, Marbled Falls, which makes it more difficult. The hike is about three-four miles one way. Many appreciate having friends with 4 x 4's meet them at the bottom end of this hike by having them drive down Gregg's Hideout Rd, then on down Hualapai Wash to Hualapai Bay at the lake, to meet hikers where they exit this canyon.

Directions

Park at the scenic overlook on Grapevine Mesa at Meadview across from the Ranger Station (just north of milepost 39 on Pearce Ferry Road). View the Old Gregg's Wagon Road to the left that leads from there on the rim and down, although note that after the old road gets down the grade and begins to level off below, it winds along a valley to the north. Right at the bottom of this grade is where you leave the Wagon Road and veer left to proceed down a wash and into Marbled Falls Canyon.

You'll approach the Dry Fall about half-way down into the canyon. I previously by-passed the falls by clambering over steep sharp rocks immediately to the right, but the last time a group went down with me, several preferred a way around the left side which required just a few careful handholds to negotiate a short drop-off before reaching the wash floor. Continue on down the wash and eventually you'll come to another broad dryfall that is easily negotiated on the right, then work your way over some sharp boulders and on down into the wash just above Hualapai Bay.

When driving the nine miles back out Hualapai Wash to reach the gravel Gregg's Hideout Road, keep your eyes open for some old faded petroglyphs on a dark outcrop of rock on the right side of the wash, just below the 'old car' that's been half submerged in the wash bed for decades.

There is extensive historical significance regarding Hualapai Wash. This was also long a prehistoric native river crossing, and later, an old ferry crossing operated there for short a time before Gregg's/Smiths Ferry was used farther north. (See book mentioned in Introduction for more information.)

Vern Farris and George Schwart at Marbled Falls, 2011

By-passing Marbled Falls

Locals standing above last dry fall approaching lake, in Marbled Falls Canyon

Faded petroglyphs alongside bed in Hualapai Wash

Turtle Rock Sink

This qualifies as a relatively easy hike only about ¼ mile one-way up a wash bed. At that point there's an interesting sink-hole I stumbled across decades ago while hiking in the hills and ridges northwest of the gravel portion of Pearce Ferry Road, the section of the road going on down to Pearce Ferry boat landing and bay. Later I took a friend back to see the curious 'pit'. With a short rope, we climbed down in and found an old skull, either of a horse or burro. The hole is not huge but is impressive, perhaps 15' at the deepest part and about 20' wide. The ceiling extends over part of the hold and could be risky to trod upon. It would be possible to hand-climb in and out of one side of the top opening as the floor is only about 8' below at that spot, except there's a small lip that makes entrance/exit somewhat difficult without rope assistance. I wrote a report on this to NPS 25 years ago, suggesting they might break that lip so exit would be more viable if something or someone fell in by mistake, but today it remains as then.

Directions

After the intersection of Pearce Ferry Road and South Cove Road, drive on down the gravel portion of Pearce Ferry road about 1.3 miles. On your right, you'll see a large rock up about 15' on the embankment that was long ago painted by someone to resemble a tortoise shell. Stop there, look back over your left shoulder and you'll see the wash that leads up to Turtle Rock Sink. As you walk up that wash you'll get to some reddish ledges and bypass a small dryfall or two. The Sink is up on the right (north) side of the wash, so you'll need to get up out of the wash to see the flat surface opening.

In years past there was a pull-out for parking near Turtle Rock but this is gone so trying to find a good place to park on Pearce Ferry road there and be out of the way is a big difficult. You might have to settle for a pull-out about a half-mile back up the gravel portion at the pull-out on the right (southeast) side.

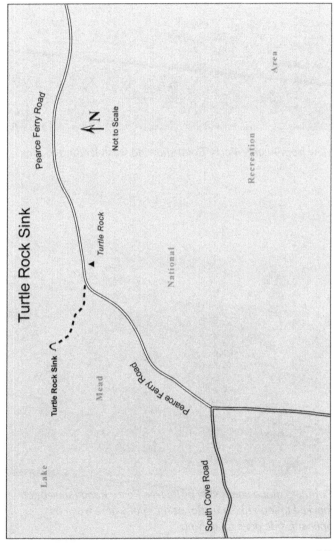

View from Pearce Ferry Road showing wash leading to Sink

Boulders along south side of Pearce Ferry Road (someone marked to look like a turtle) at the spot where wash on opposite side goes up to Sink

Vern climbing into Sink Hole

Vern inspecting floor of Sink

Vern climbing out of Sink Hole

Section Two: Grapevine Mesa East

This section includes several hikes leading off the mesa on the east side and others down in Grapevine Wash, the long major drainage laying between Grapevine Mesa and tall escarpment of Grand Wash Cliffs to the east. Hidden within Grapevine Wash is Grapevine Springs, a beautiful historic oasis and namesake for this entire expanse of mesa and wash.

The Grand Wash Cliffs, a great escarpment of sheer cliffs, form the eastern horizon from Meadview and Grapevine Mesa. \These Cliffs are impressive in their own right and are the western-most edge of the vast high Colorado Plateau country present in our southwestern states.

Ancient Roasting Pits and Seep

This is an interesting and relatively easy walk into the midst of Grapevine Wash. Located there are two excellent examples of huge roasting pits that Native Americans once used throughout this area when roasting parts of various plants in the Yucca family.

Directions

Find approved back road #145 that leaves Meadview from the south end of the most eastern-located road, Shore Avenue. This is a 4 x 4 trail that splits in short order, one branch going off to the right taking you down into an unnamed wash, then northerly to pass near the Lucky Seven Corral. The other route takes you down closer by the corral, then rejoins the previous route mentioned. The Lucky Seven Corral (named for section seven) and windmill was put in by ranchers in the mid- 50's for livestock watering. When the community of Meadview was developed not long after, a number of original residents who had property without water drove down here to fill up their water wagons. By 2000, the windmill had broken down and no more water was pumped, the large old trees there soon died and recently have been cut down.

After you pass the corral, continue northerly in that wash just a short distance. Off to the right, keep an eye out for a low hill, one that has NPS 'no motor vehicle' stakes posted on an old trail that goes up a hill. Park at the bottom, park and walk up and you'll find a seep that was long-used by Indians, one a rancher dubbed 'Cramp Springs'. The huge old tree has been there for decades. I once crawled into the low cave spring source and pulled out the rotting carcass of a bobcat. After checking out this seep, continue walking eastward, following various livestock trails that meander over several more hills. Watch for two large roasting pits in a low area, just before you get to the larger main Grapevine Wash drainage.

In the 1980's there were problems with a local driving a dirt bike through these roasting pits and I suggested to NPS that they might want to fence them. They did and provided a walk-through. The fencing makes these pits a bit easier to locate when on the ridge above.

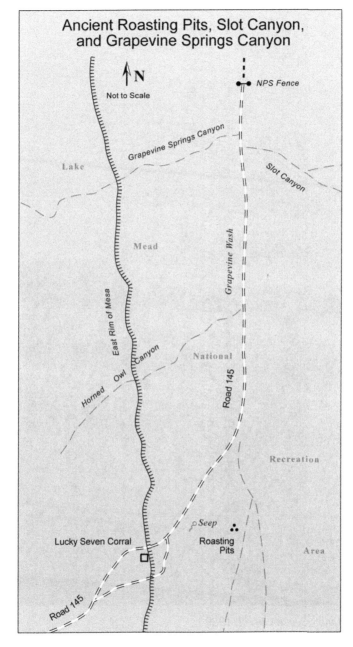

Ancient Roasting Pits, Slot Canyon, and Grapevine Springs Canyon

Lucky Seven Corral, 1989

The seep at Cramp Springs, 2009

One of the ancient Roasting Pits, 2009

Horned Owl Canyon

This is an easy to moderate hike, with several dryfalls involved but by-passing them is not difficult. The canyon is about 2-3 miles long. It's nice to have someone meet you with a 4x4 at the lower end and take you on down to historic Grapevine Springs in Grapevine Wash, then drive back out to Meadview.

I also found this during the 1980's, although with it's close proximity to Meadview and Grapevine Wash, I'm sure others had hiked down through it previously . The first time I walked through this canyon and while traversing through a narrows, two Horned Owls took flight, thus the name. The next time I went through there were three Horned Owlet babies in a nest on one ledge. On hikes after 2000, I saw no more owls. Some groups that hiked this during later years have called it Marble Canyon, but this tends to then get confused with Marbled Falls Canyon off the other side of the mesa.

Directions

There is a deep wash that goes through the east side of Meadview, just below the Meadview Civic Center or east of Haystack drive. In the 80's, we simply called this large wash the 'Pit Wash' because there was a large gravel pit in operation there (now moved farther south, same wash). Walk down that wash and as it takes you northeasterly, you'll come to a nice broad dryfall which can be easily bypassed but which conveniently keeps ATV's from accessing this particular canyon. Then the wash narrows and becomes a more interesting canyon to walk. As you approach the lower end, a large deep dryfall will appear but this can also be bypassed on the left. This one keeps ATV's from accessing this canyon from the lower end so the dryfalls in this canyon insure that it is preserved for hikers who want a quiet beautiful place to visit.

Upon exiting Horned Owl Canyon, you'll come out into the larger Grapevine Wash. If you have no ride, you can turn right and hike back up Grapevine Wash and to the Lucky

Seven Corral and back up to Meadview.   Or, you can turn left at that exit and hike on down to Grapevine Springs and Grapevine Springs Canyon.

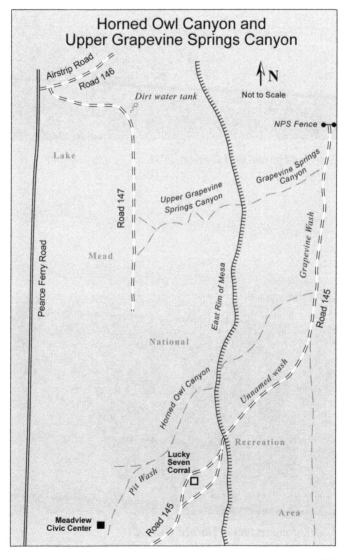

Entering Horned Owl Canyon, 2011

Local group resting in Horned Owl, 2011

Upper Grapevine Springs Canyon

This is the beautiful upper part of Grapevine Springs Canyon. A large dryfall difficult to get around separates this part from the lower part where Grapevine Springs is actually located so most hikers prefer to hike down to the dryfall, then turn around and hike back out. This hike is about four miles long, depending how far one goes before turning around.

Directions

While still up on Grapevine Mesa, drive north from the scenic overlook a little over four miles on Pearce Ferry Road to the gravel airport road turn-off (approved back road #146), turn there and then immediately right on another approved back road, #147 (this road often requires either a high-rise or 4 x 4 vehicle). This will take you easterly past a large old dirt water tank, then curve back south. When you see what looks like a wash or cut opening to the east (left), park your vehicle and hike in (there are two entrances forming a 'y', that go into Upper Grapevine Springs Canyon... you can enter either).

You'll soon do a little rock climbing around a medium drop-off, then began winding your way on down through a magnificent canyon that gets deeper and more impressive as you go. In some places you may want to take time to explore slots and caverns that have formed in massive fallen boulders on the canyon floor. After walking several miles through scenic canyon walls, you'll come to a very narrow area and then the dryfall that is impassable for most hikers without the use of a rope. Look over the edge and you'll see greenery below, and if quiet, may hear water running. Grapevine Springs is located in that lush greenery. To reach that area, most hike in via Lower Grapevine Spring Canyon, from Grapevine Wash, the large drainage below.

Sharon descending first dry fall area, 2005

Granite Dells in Upper Canyon, 1998

Layered wall in Upper Canyon where dry fall is located right above Grapevine Springs source below

Rock cavern and dry fall in Upper Grapevine Springs Canyon

Another cavern area in Upper Grapevine Springs Canyon

Rock crevasse area in Upper Grapevine Springs Canyon

Lower Grapevine Springs Canyon

This favorite canyon has long been a draw for humans. It is a very historic place, as is the entire drainage of Grapevine Wash. The area was a prehistoric trade route used for centuries by Indians to cross around the western end of Grand Canyon, one called 'The Old Ute Trail'. This historic trail came from Utah and headed south, eventually hooking in with the Old Mojave Indian Trail that ran from east to west in Arizona and crossed into California. Although the old river crossing here (at the north end of Grapevine Wash) of the Colorado River was not easy at what later became known as Pearce Ferry, Grapevine Wash, itself, was a good historic travel route. Grapevine Springs (earlier known as Paiute name, Dinbah), some six miles or so from the river, was a fine water source and resting place, then in another six-seven miles, travelers came to Grass Springs (historically known as Tinaka, then later, Diamond Bar Ranch, now Grand Canyon West Ranch), another fine water source and resting place. (For far more historic information see my former published work, A Deep Map of Western Grand Canyon and Upper Lake Mead available at Meadview Chamber of Commerce or on Amazon.)

Directions

You will need a 4 x 4 to drive from Meadview on approved back road #145 (off the eastern-most road in Meadview, Shore Ave) and down into Grapevine Wash as the wash bed usually has very sandy areas where it's easy to get bogged down. This little road splits just as you go down, one route taking you past the old Lucky Seven Corral, the other by-passing the corral around the south, but both routes soon re-join and take you northerly down this unnamed wash and then into the adjoining larger Grapevine Wash. Grapevine Springs Canyon is about three miles or so farther north in Grapevine Wash.

After driving some distance, you'll see a canyon opening coming in on the left, which is the Horned Owl Canyon mentioned elsewhere in this information. Keep going another mile or so with an eye for some shrubs and desert greenery in another opening to the left. This is Grapevine Springs Canyon. If you reach the NPS fence across Grapevine Wash, you've gone a bit too far.

Park at the mouth of the canyon and you'll probably see water coming out onto the floor of the main wash. Walk up into the shrubbery on a trail of sorts on the north (right) side and it will take you through a walk-through gate. Follow that trail into the canyon entrance. Keep your eyes open. On the left side across the water, you can find what I called Signature Wall which contains many old historic pioneer signatures. One black signature is easily visible from a distance, 'J Judd 1883', but there are many more scratched into that wall. Some of this wall caved in during a flash flood in this canyon in the 90's, but many names are still present.

If you continue to follow the water you will come to the first pond and hardier hikers will want to go on up to the second one. Some even struggle on up through the brush and water to try to get to the spring source, itself, but that takes extended effort.

In addition to a huge flash flood that came through Grapevine Springs Canyon in the early 1990's and washed out both ponds, changing the terrain greatly, just a few years ago another huge flash flood came down the greater Grapevine Wash, depositing much of the debris currently present at the mouth of Grapevine Springs Canyon.

*National Park Service sign and fence in Grapevine Wash,
just north of entrance to Grapevine Springs Canyon*

*Grapevine Springs Canyon Hike… showing entrance to
Canyon from Grapevine Wash*

Upper pond as pictured in 1986

Locals enjoying Upper Pond and falls in Grapevine Springs Canyon

Oldest of the historic signatures on Signature Wall, 1986

Another historic signature on Signature Wall in Grapevine Springs Canyon

Lower falls and pond as seen in 2010

Another view of the lower pond

Slot Canyon

Years ago I called this Slot Canyon because of the slot-like entrance, however, some of this entrance caved in making the 'slot' not so distinct. This hike is not designated on the map but the opening is located almost right across the wash from the opening to Grapevine Springs Canyon and takes one back up toward the Grand Wash Cliffs. It splits into two branches with one going toward what locals call the 'dryfall' located about halfway up the cliff face. Local hikers have recently been calling this Lost Cable Canyon due to an old cable remaining high on one side. Since this is a round trip, it is approximately six miles or so... depending how far one wants to go.

Directions

Drive from Meadview and down approved back road #145 into Grapevine Wash, and use a 4 x 4 as the sand in this wash bed can often bog one down. Drive several miles or so in Grapevine Wash and just before reaching the entrance on the left into Grapevine Springs Canyon, there's an opening on the right (east, toward Grand Wash Cliffs) into a canyon.

Discrepancies in Maps from Other Sources

For clarification, I would like to mention some puzzling discrepancies that exist in area maps available from other sources.

The 2008 version of the Lake Mead Recreation Area Approved Back Roads map calls the entire lengthy Grapevine Wash drainage east of Meadview, 'Grapevine Canyon', as also does the 2010 version of the Benchmark Arizona Road and Recreation Atlas. In contrast, all other published maps, government maps, historic maps, historic sources, and knowledge of locals of which I'm aware have always called this Grapevine Wash. Only the smaller side canyon of Grapevine Springs Canyon was called 'canyon'.

The 2002 version of the Bureau of Land Management map of the north half of Kingman Area District showing this area, has the old historic site of Tinaka Springs in the wrong place, having moved it from the former Diamond Bar Ranch/now Grand Canyon West Ranch and up into Iron Basin farther south. This error probably occurred as there is a benchmark high on Iron Mountain called 'Tinaka' and this was designated such on some older maps as surveyors often placed these at high points named after sites nearby. Apparently this benchmark name was recently misinterpreted as a spring and misplaced for this reason.

In addition, some of the real estate maps available at Meadview and Lake Mead City call the Grapevine Mesa rim on the west (at the scenic overlook on Pearce Ferry Road), 'Grapevine Canyon Rim', which seems illogical since Grapevine Canyon is located, instead, on the east side of Grapevine Mesa. This error had apparently been perpetuated from when it was misnamed on one of the old real estate promotional maps for this area in the 1960's.

Made in the USA
Middletown, DE
14 October 2022